EGYPT, ASSYRIA, ISRAEL AND THEIR GOD

Wordflowers

Woodbridge, Virginia

Dake's Annotated Reference Bible, The Holy Bible, Containing the Old and New Testaments of the King James Version Text by Finis Jennings Dake, Dake Bible Sales, Inc. Lawrenceville, Georgia 30246, December 1993, all rights reserved.

Unless otherwise noted, "Vocabulary Definitions at the end of book are quoted from The Merriam-Webster Dictionary and also Vines & Strong's Concise Biblical Dictionary,"

New International Version, Women of Faith Study Bible, by The Zondervan Corporation, Grand Rapids, Michigan, 49530, Copyright 2001, all rights reserved.

The Holy Bible, New Century Version, by Word Publishing, a division of Thomas Nelson, Inc., Copyright 1991, All rights reserved.

Scripture taken from the *New King James Version.* © Copyright 1982 by Thomas Nelson, Inc. Used by permission. All rights reserved.

Special Thank you to Tania Rawat & Tania Arts for her Illustrative Designs. *The illustrative Design in Chapter 2 was created by Wordflowers. The illustrative Design in Chapter 3 was found online at: www.ask-aladin.com/culture1.htm*
Internet World Wide Web Resources:
http://en.wikipedia.org/wiki/Social_life_in_Babylonia_and_Assyria

©Egypt, Assyria, Israel and their God
ISBN-10: **0-9886403-6-8**
ISBN-13: **978-0-9886403-6-8**
©Egypt, Assyria, Israel and their God
Published by The Wordflowers Corporation
also known as ®Wordflowers
Copyright© 2013 ®Wordflowers

Library of Congress Control Number: **2013915463**

Your questions, inquiries, and requests for more information are welcome at: info@wordflowerscorp.org. You may also visit our website at www.wordflowerscorp.org. You may also call us at (571)-232-9122 or you may write to us at:

Wordflowers
Post Office Box 406
Occoquan, Virginia 22125

Printed and distributed in the United States of America and Internationally. All rights reserved under International Copyright Law. No part of this book may be reproduced or transmitted in any form or by any means, electronic or mechanical, including photocopying, recording, or by any information storage and retrieval system, without the written permission of the publisher.

Dedication

"This book is dedicated to Yahweh, our Great and Mighty God who loves and cares for us and our nations both affectionately and watchfully. Thank you for your love O Lord!"

Table of Contents

CHAPTER	PAGE
Introduction: *Believing Nations Abide in Love*	7
ONE: Through Jesus	11
TWO: Egypt	17
THREE: Egyptian Culture	21
FOUR: The Assyrian Rule	25
FIVE: The Israelites and their culture	29
SIX: Reconciliation of the Nations	37
PRAYER OF SALVATION	39
ABOUT THE AUTHOR	41
Vocabulary Words	43
Notes	45

Introduction

BELIEVING NATIONS ABIDE IN LOVE

The nations symbolize you and me. Just like us kids struggle to find meaning and purpose in life, so do nations. For centuries nations have sought to find a God who can be connected with something tangible or visible. The ancient people often carved idols out of wood and images were worshipped and exalted as God. The ancient people did not Believe. I'm a Believer, and I Believe!

Yahweh is Israel's sacred name for God and it means LORD. Yahweh is LORD who is able to work miracles so that all may believe and trust in Him. Yahweh's guiding presence led the Israelites with a cloud by day and fire by night.

"And the Lord went before them by day in a pillar of a cloud, to lead them the way; and by night in a pillar of *fire, to give them light; to go by day and night: He took not away the pillar of the cloud by day, nor the pillar of fire by night, from before the people (Exodus 13:21-22 KJV)."*

Yahweh can do the impossible because HE IS God. Although we cannot "see" Yahweh, we believe in Him by faith. Through His creation, we see and sense Him.

Let's ponder the works of the Lord! God has given us eyes and ears to see and listen. We see birds and trees! We see each other! God has blessed us with a dwelling, a home to rest and study. God provides us with food and clothes because

He loves us. He takes care of everything we could ever need or desire. God says that if we delight ourselves in Him, He will give us the desires of our heart.

The Apostle John says that we must know and believe the Love GOD has for us; for GOD is Love and he who abides in Love, abides in GOD and GOD in him (I John 4:16). This is proof that GOD is within you and me! His Kingdom is within you and me (Luke 17:21)! That is why we must abide in love.

JESUS IS THE WAY

CHAPTER 1

THROUGH JESUS

Despite doing bad things and not seeing 'eye to eye' with Yahweh's Word, Yahweh loves humanity and desires **fellowship** with all people. A **fellowship** is a partnership, a companionship, a sharing, and participation where two or more people support each other in every way. Noah was the first man who habitually fellowshipped with God. Noah found grace in the eyes of the Lord and he did all that God commanded him in building an ark to save humanity (Gen. 6:8). Today, all Believers are called into the fellowship of God's Son **Yeshua**. He is our Lord who died to save humanity from sin and all of its effects (1 Cor. 1:9; 2 Cor. 5:21). Now we are **the Righteousness of God**: we are approved and acceptable and in right relationship with Him by His goodness. This is also Yahweh's Love for every nation! Through Yahweh's Son Yeshua, diverse nations that oppose the

God of Israel can become reconciled to Yahweh and receive His support in every way. We all belong to Yahweh and Yahweh loves to teach and help us to know Him; to know Him is to know what is right. Yahweh loves us despite our rebellion. Likewise Yahweh Loves the nations as His own children despite their rebellion (Isaiah 19:25) but He hates the sin.

    Religious traditions that were taught to the people of Israel through their leaders were passed down and commanded by Yahweh to be taught from generation to generation (Deut. 4:9-10). Yet Yahweh decided to come closer to us so that we may see Him as He really is! Yahweh did this by manifesting Himself in the form of a man known as **Yeshua**! **Yeshua** is Yahweh's only begotten Son. Yeshua's Greek name is **Jesus** and through Jesus we have become sons and daughters of Yahweh! We have become **the righteousness of God** and we are accepted in the beloved! Through **Jesus**, the nations are also Yahweh's sons and daughters and through **Jesus** they are also **the Righteousness of God** and

accepted in the beloved!

CHAPTER 2

EGYPT

Let's STUDY the nation of Egypt! Covering the face of their land, the Egyptians are a powerful demographic of people who have been delivered and are settled (Numbers 22:5-6). Yahweh's Word shows us that Egypt was a place of abundance; palaces were erected complete with land for sheep and cattle; male and female donkeys; men servants and maid servants; and camel (Gen. 12:10). The Israelites were an abundant nation also; they were exceedingly numerous, fruitful and multiplied greatly; so much so that they were feared by the Egyptians. This made Egypt a place of oppression and bondage for the Israelites (Exodus 3:7).

  Pharaoh, the oppressive ruler, had repeatedly been commanded by Yahweh to release the people of Israel (Exodus 7:16

NCV). After many acts of judgment by Yahweh, such as the plague of blood, the plague of frogs, and the plague of gnats, to no avail Pharaoh insisted that the people of Israel be subject to His oppressive rule (Exodus 7 - 8; Exodus 8:32; 8:19).

Yahweh released Israel out of Egypt by sequential disasters. One by one Pharaoh began to see things Yahweh's way.

"When Pharaoh stubbornly refused to let us go, the Lord killed every firstborn in Egypt, both man and animal. This is why I sacrifice to the Lord the first male offspring of every womb and redeem each of my firstborn sons (Exodus 13:15)."

Other unfavorable judgments were also caused by years of practicing idolatry and disobedience to Yahweh and His ways.

> "The Egyptians will lose heart, and I will bring their plans to nothing. They will consult the idols and the spirits of the dead, the mediums and the spiritists. I will hand the Egyptians over to the power of a cruel master, and a fierce king will rule over them," declares the Lord, the Lord Almighty (Isaiah 19:3-4)."

CHAPTER 3

Egyptian Culture

Entrenched in Egyptian culture during the Biblical era was the polytheistic belief of other gods. For example, many Egyptians worshipped the bull god *Apis*, the goddess *Isis* and the ram god *Khnum* who are associated with "the power and blessing" of the Nile River. The Nile was the Egyptians only source of water. The Nile was often called the bloodstream of Osiris. Osiris was considered the god of earth and vegetation who turned arid desert into fertile land. Thus Osiris was often credited by the Egyptians of causing crops to grow and animals to be reared. The Egyptians did not recognize that it was actually the Lord who caused the waters to spring up and flow through the Nile. It was the Lord who said because of their defiant disobedience the waters would fail from the Nile and the river would become wasted and become dry (Isaiah 19:4-5). The Egyptian's rebellion, defiance, and trust in other gods grieved the Lord who states His requirements to living:

"The Lord has told you human, what is good; he has told you what he wants from you: to do what is right to other people, love being kind to others, and live humbly, obeying your God. (Micah 6:8 NCV)."

Today, out of Egypt's 71 million populace, 62 million Egyptians are Sunni Muslims and approximately 8 million are Christian Egyptians. Egyptian society is largely founded on Middle Eastern family traditions derived from various religious rules of Christianity and Islam.

CHAPTER 4

The Assyrian's Rule

The Assyrian Empire, founded by Asshur the son of Shem (Gen. 10:11, 22), is known for its organized military power and autocratic rulers. Once enemies of the Israelites, whom they oppressed for over 175 years, they were characterized as ravaging lions.

"Israel is like scattered sheep; the lions have driven him away. First the King of Assyria devoured him; now at last this Nebuchadnezzar King of Babylon has broken his bones (Jer. 50:17)."

Assyria is also known as Syria and its ancient name is **Khor**. Historically, the origin of the Assyrian people date back to pre-Islamic Mesopotamia during the Akkadian Empire. Notably, it was during the 1st to 3rd centuries in Roman Syria and Persian Assyria that the Assyrians became Christians. During the 5th century through the 8th century, some converted to Islam after the Islamic conquest of Mesopotamia. Religious and ethnic persecution is prevalent in recent Assyrian history. At the onset of WWI, the Assyrian genocide caused massive persecution. This caused the Assyrians to resettle to other countries such as Syria, **Persia** (present day Iran), Iraq and other neighboring countries near the Middle East.

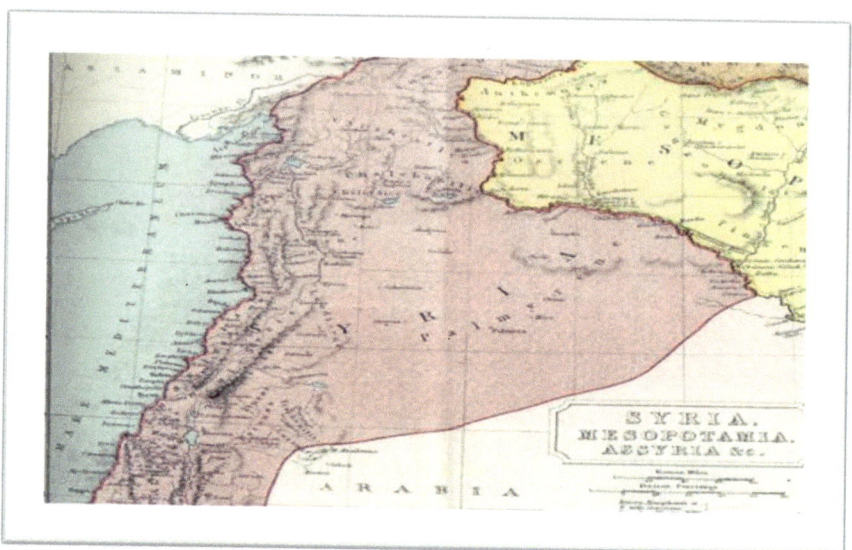

Map of Ancient Syria. From The Atlas of Ancient and Classical Geography, by Samuel Butler, Ernest Rhys, editor (1907, repr. 1908). *From The Atlas of Ancient and Classical Geography, by Samuel Butler, Ernest Rhys, ed.*

CHAPTER 5

The Israelites and their Tribes

Once called a trickster, Yahweh favored **Jacob** and renamed him Israel, Yahweh's Prince! The tribes of Israel were named after Jacob's twelve sons: Reuben, Simeon, Levi, Judah, Dan, Naphtali, Gad, Asher, Issachar, Zebulun, Joseph and Benjamin. The tribe of Judah brought the lineage of Jesus through King David whose ancestry continues today and forever more (Psalm 89:3, 29, 36)!

"Abraham was the father of Isaac, Isaac the father of Jacob, Jacob the father of Judah and his brothers...So all the generations from Abraham to David are fourteen, from David to the Babylonian exile fourteen generations, from the Babylonian exile to the Christ fourteen generations (Matthew 1:2,17)".

The Israelites are called Yahweh's chosen people and were commanded to follow Yahweh's law and ways. When Yahweh's law became difficult to keep and the Israelites became repeatedly rebellious, Yahweh's preordained plan to free them from the bondage of sin brought Yahweh's mercy and grace. Yahweh knew this was necessary because He is THE Beginning (Alpha) and THE End (Omega) and He SEES beforehand! Through His Son Jesus all people can now live under GRACE!

During Biblical times the priest offered sacrifices for the sins of the people. The person who broke Yahweh's command had to bring a sacrifice such as an animal, turtledove, or pigeon. Symbolically, the person's sin was then applied to the animal, turtledove, or pigeon. An unblemished ox, bull, or sheep was considered a costly and high sacrifice, while grain, a turtledove or pigeon was considered a less costly sacrifice. Sacrifice is a matter of the heart. Sometimes Yahweh did not receive the high sacrifices of the people because they sacrificed out of requirement and not from a heart of love for Him. Stubbornly they continued in their sin but did not turn away from their sin and be changed from their heart (**Repentance**).

After the animal was brought to the priest it was sacrificed at the altar where its blood was sprinkled at all four corners and the priest then washed at a large fountain filled with water CALLED A **LAVAR**. THE PRIEST THEN entered the tabernacle to worship. The Holies of Holies was the meeting place for only the priest and Yahweh. This is where the needs of the people where made known to Yahweh. The Holies of Holies contained the Ark of the Covenant. The Ark of the Covenant was rectangular shaped and made of pure gold. On each side of the top of the Ark were stationed two gold cherubim's whose faces were covered by its wings because of the sacredness of Yahweh's presence. Today, each person can go to Yahweh for themselves without bringing an animal, grain, turtledove or pigeon to the priest to be sacrificed for sin. Now Jesus' blood gives us immediate access to Yahweh for forgiveness. Through Jesus everyone can go to Yahweh in Jesus' Name. This is because Yahweh sent Jesus to die as the **propitiation** for all sin (to reconcile every person and bring peace between Yahweh and man). Jesus purchased our souls with His life (His blood). Before Jesus came the priest was the **mediator** between Yahweh and man. Today, Yahweh wants everyone to believe in Him and His Son! Yahweh brought Jesus to earth and Jesus lived, died, and Yahweh resurrected Him and Jesus now lives! Yahweh wants everyone to pray in Jesus' name because Jesus is the **mediator** between Yahweh and man. A **mediator** is someone who mediates between two parties with the view to produce peace. The freedom and safety (**salvation**) of humanity was secured by Jesus when He offered Himself by dying on the cross and rising from death.

CHAPTER 6

RECONCILIATION OF THE NATIONS

"In that day there will be a highway from Egypt to Assyria. The Assyrians will go to Egypt and the Egyptians to Assyria. The Egyptians and Assyrians will worship together. In that day Israel will be the third, along with Egypt and Assyria, a blessing on the earth. The Lord Almighty will bless them, saying, "Blessed be Egypt my people, Assyria my handiwork, and Israel my inheritance (Isaiah 19:23- 25)."

This prophecy of Scripture foretold in Isaiah will manifest for the nations. Jesus brought about this reconciliation! Although it is not manifested everywhere in the world our faith and hope in Yahweh causes us to believe. Jesus was slain before the foundation of the world and sealed believers by the gift of the Holy Spirit. When the nations believe in Yahweh and His Son Jesus, a **regeneration** or new birth of nations begins. This act of believing secures Yahweh's promise of the Holy Spirit for the nations. Faith in Yahweh brings peace to the nations!

Prayer of Salvation

Dear Yahweh, I believe in you and the Love you have for me. I repent of my sin and I invite your Son Jesus into my heart. I receive the forgiveness you died to give me. I confess with my mouth and I believe in my heart that You are Lord (Romans 10:10-13). I pray Shalom, your great peace, over my life and over the nations. I pray that others may receive Jesus also. I am saved and I am a Believer and I Believe You and Your Word (Romans 10:10-15; Isaiah 55:11 KJV)! In Jesus Name I pray. Amen.

About the Author:

Ms. Misha Grace Benjamin is the Founder and President of The Wordflowers Corporation. Wordflowers is a Christian Publishing Company that speaks and distinctively praises God's Word in the earth. At Wordflowers, Ms. Benjamin is also a Writer and Author who specializes in Christian and Children's Literature. Ms. Benjamin is a graduate of the Institute of Children's Literature. Ms. Benjamin also works as a Volunteer Teacher for English Speakers of Other Languages (ESOL) and also as a Children's Story-Time Reader. Ms. Benjamin currently resides in Woodbridge, VA.

KEY VOCABULARY WORDS

Yahweh: God's name which means Lord.

Fellowship: a partnership, a sharing and participation where two or more people support each other in every way.

Yeshua: Jesus' Hebrew name.

The Righteousness of God: To be upright and in right standing with God. All Christians are the righteousness of God.

Jesus: Yeshua's Greek name.

Khor: Syria's ancient name.

Persia: Present day Iran.

REPENTANCE: To turn away from your sin and be changed from your heart.

LAVAR: a large fountain filled with water.

MEDIATOR: someone who mediates between two parties with the view to produce peace.

PROPITIATION: to reconcile every person and bring peace between Yahweh and man.

REGENERATION: New Birth

SALVATION: Freedom and safety

Jacob: Isaac's son whose name means Trickster whom God renamed Israel.

Notes for Discussion:

Notes for Discussion:

Notes for Discussion:

Notes for Discussion:

Notes for Discussion:

Notes for Discussion:

Notes for Discussion:

Notes for Discussion:

Notes for Discussion:

Notes for Discussion:

Notes for Discussion: